**Other work by Julien Bouchard
At Trafford Publishing**

Discoveries through meditation

Meditation,
A way of life...

JULIEN BOUCHARD

Order this book online at www.trafford.com
or email orders@trafford.com

Most Trafford titles are also available at major online book retailers.

Printed in the United States of America.

ISBN: 978-1-4669-4693-4 (sc)
ISBN: 978-1-4669-4692-7 (e)

Trafford rev. 07/05/2012

 www.trafford.com

North America & international
toll-free: 1 888 232 4444 (USA & Canada)
phone: 250 383 6864 ♦ fax: 812 355 4082

TABLE OF CONTENTS

Meditation, a way of life . . .

to relax,
to reduce stress,
to improve your concentration,
to improve your performance,
to speed-up your healing,
to find answer to your questions,
to experience peace,
to center your life,
to live harmoniously,
to live happily with yourself
and more . . .

Julien Bouchard
Sherrington, Québec
Canada
julien@julienbouchard.com
www.julienbouchard.com

To Paramahansa the Kagyütpa

Beyond the beyond . . .

Body and mind totally relaxed
Without effort, flexible as nature
Break the yoke of the runaway thought process
Ready to jump over the great wall
Then one must open the doors of the wind
On which rhythm is resting
Then open wide the vents
And push the wind down to the guts
Let the air follow its course
Set your inside view on emptiness
Concentrate on silence without effort
Forget your body and listen to the present
Master the dynamics of your thought process
Break through the latent mirror
To reach the unique moment
That will allow you to transcend the present
The absence of timeless distractions
The light of the cosmic infinity
The wisdom expanding in time
The moment has become one
If from the bottom of emptiness without distinction
The mind without effort observes the mind
The observed becomes the alert observer
It becomes possible to touch freedom

Julien Bouchard

GENERAL

WHAT MEDITATION IS

> *"I must use clairvoyance and powers obtained through meditation to assist people in understanding MahaMudra."*
>
> *Garmapa Rangjang Dorje*

Wise men of all times defined the practice of meditation in tens and maybe hundreds of different ways, always according to their own philosophical method and school.

But after in-depth analysis of various meditation practices and techniques our final deduction is that it consists in a sole and always similar procedure, which is the FIXATION OF THE ATTENTION ON A UNIQUE THING (thought, breathing, mantra, object, etc.) WHILE REMAINING ALERT TO ANY OCCURRENCES WITHOUT ANALYSIS, the concentration of the consciousness on a unique goal without distraction while being totally alert without analysis, the adept becomes the observer. In order to reach this state, some use different tools; some set their attention on a sound, a mental image, an object, a thought, a word, breathing, emptiness, etc. But anyone, by means of these various supports and exercises is trying to understand the nature of thoughts and to develop a power of attention sufficiently strong on the first hand to ignore the emerging and immersing process of thoughts due to the cerebral mechanism and on the other hand while experimenting a state of total relaxation and mental silence to eventually make contact with the essence of the inner self.

Meditation is a mental state in which the practitioner, totally relaxed of body and mind, does not think or analyze anything, he only observes without defining anything. The state of consciousness and attention of the meditator will, with time, become total, without any distraction.

Meditation allows one to discover a unique state in our bipolar universe, a state that is stable, does not change, cannot be modified, altered or aged. A stable and permanent state that it is always possible to find identical, unmodified. SILENCE, EMPTINESS WITHOUT DISTRACTION which is meditation prompting inner silence becomes a refuge against confusion, uncertainty and suffering. This is also a discipline that allows one to uncover the secrets of being human, his reason for being here and his role within the great creation scheme.

The silence of mental emptiness, that only meditation can provide, is the only thing or state that will not change, will not be modified or transformed in the world of duality in which we are all immersed. This is the only stable data that will never be altered in any ways. The silence of mental emptiness is the same today that it will be tomorrow; it was

the same a thousand years ago and it will be the same in ten thousand years from now. Everything else, without exception in this world is modified, transformed to become something else. We are born to age, we build today to see our creations come apart, change and finally disappear. We understand these various states differently according to our culture and our current grasp of events, including the interpretation of the state of meditation, but the inner silence, product of meditation will always be the same for all.

Meditation, as well as its results, is personal experiences that only the meditator can grasp and understand. Only one's own meditation experiences can bring awareness and truth. The experiences of others in this field, positive as they can be, have no value for a third party other than at the information level. The experiences of others cannot bring you the truth, they can only be taken as advice and give one good reasons to meditate and in this way find out what it means to discover oneself through one's own meditating experiences.

Meditation is a body and mind relaxation process in which one's consciousness and attention are total, thus the never ending dance of thoughts no longer affects the meditator. The stimulus caused by emerging and immersing thoughts having disappeared, the meditator rests in a state of total mental peace and tranquillity.

Tilopa, a great Indian wise man who lived around the 10th century was singing the fine quality of "MahaMudra", the Great Symbol, one of the oldest and purest form of meditation that was originally expounded by a master named Saraha as early as the first century BC and even then, he was claiming that the Great

Symbol was already very old. It is said that MahaMudra could go back as far as Siddharta Gautama himself around 566 BC and perhaps even before then. This meditation technique is still practiced in the East as well as in the West through the adepts of Kagyütpa.

"Do not do anything but relax your body, do not talk, do not pray, remain silent, empty your mind of thoughts and think of nothing, contemplate emptiness. As the blade of grass bending to the wind, let your body rest. MahaMudra is like a spirit free of any attachment. By thus practicing, with time, you will become wise . . ."

After 2500 years these words are as current as the latest electronic gadget launched on the market.

WHAT MEDITATION IS NOT

People have a tendency to interpret, to understand what is out of their field of experience, and this is totally normal. The nature of man is to catalogue things, experiences, insert them into small compartments in order to feel in control of what is happening in his surroundings. Otherwise he feels inadequate, insecure and vulnerable facing what he has not perfectly identified and classified within his mental archives.

The same phenomenon arises with meditation's experiences that one has analyzed, weighed and classified in several ways, and the reason for this short chapter is to ensure that you understand that meditation is not some interpretations more or less accurate of what it really is.

Meditation is not analytical thinking, meditation is not mental release, nor autosuggestion and even less a state of dreaming, half sleep or self-hypnosis.

Meditation is not a religion, nor a sect!

FOUNDATIONS OF MEDITATION

> *"Each human being is his own prison. But each one can also acquire the power to escape from it . . ."*
>
> *Siddharta Gautama Buddha*

Meditation goes back to the beginning of humanity and well before the birth of Siddhartha Gautama (Buddha) who was born around 566 BC in India.

Meditation appeared the day one person, for the first time, became aware that his or her suffering subsided when they stopped thinking about it. Afterward that person realized that each time they established inner silence, they was no longer any influence from the endless noisy thinking process, even when silence remained only for a short period, they felt a state of peace and calm unequaled any other ways. They came out of this state more serene and less affected by the cause of suffering, that could be relegated to a second plan. It is from this overwhelming discovery that masters and Siddhartha Gautama himself stated and preached the four following truths to the world:

1. LIFE LEADS AUTOMATICALLY TO SUFFERING

> *The first noble truth regarding suffering*
>
> *"Birth is suffering, old age is suffering, disease is suffering, death is suffering, being united to one that one dislikes is suffering, being separated from a loved one is suffering, not being able to realize what one desires is suffering, everything leads to suffering one way or another."*
>
> *Buddha*

Life cannot exist without desire, all forms of life and consciousness cannot exist without desire. Nothing can exist if the desire to exist is not present. Therefore our life is based on desire (want) and it is possible that one's desires cannot be fulfilled (thus pain, grief/suffering). We also wish to keep what we have acquired (desire to retain), and we can also lose this (thus pain and suffering). All forms of suffering rest on these two possibilities, the desire to acquire what we desire and the desire to retain what we have acquired.

2. SUFFERING IS ROOTED IN DESIRE

> *The second noble truth regarding suffering*
>
> *"The desire to re-exist or the wish to come back to life, is related to a passionate avidity to find new enjoyment, once here, once there, meaning the thirst for sensual pleasures, the thirst for existence and becoming, and the thirst for the non-existence."*
>
> *Buddha*

Our whole life is based on two basic factors, gain and loss. First there is the desire to live, then to possess, furthermore not to lose what we have acquired, and finally not lose life itself. Suffering can be summarized by the following: the impossibility to acquire what we want and the loss of what we have acquired. And, what we call happiness of course is the reverse, acquiring what we desire and keeping what we have acquired.

3. IT IS POSSIBLE TO AVOID SUFFERING BY REDUCING THE SCOPE OF ONE'S DESIRE

The third noble truth regarding the reduction of suffering

"To completely terminate this thirst, one must leave it behind, ignore it, free oneself from it, separate oneself from it."

Buddha

A person who has no desire, who does not wish to acquire anything, cannot lose anything; there is no desire to fulfill one way or another. There is nothing to gain or lose.

This position is very upsetting for people of an era where pseudo happiness is uniquely based on the possession of wealth. The formula can be more acceptable if it is expressed as follows: "It is possible to reduce suffering by reducing the desire to acquire or possess."

Desire is like a large leaking pail that one has to continuously refill. We fill the pail of our desires with the things that we believe will bring us happiness, after some time, we become tired of our acquisitions, the pail is leaking and new desires come to fore that we believe we have to fulfill to reach happiness again. When there is no desire, there is no pail to fill. When one's desire is less important, the pail is not as large and leaks it contents more slowly.

But to eliminate one's desire does not necessarily mean that we cannot possess anything anymore, quite the contrary. It means that we can possess anything we like but **WIHTOUT BEING ATTACHED TO IT**. This is a big difference.

Happiness rests on our acknowledgment of the facts mentioned above; when we realize that we cannot obtain everything we desire and keep everything that we wish to keep. The sole fact to be conscious that we cannot obtain everything we want and keep everything we have gained allows us to view differently all gains and losses that one experiences through life.

Meditation allows one to realize that inner happiness and peace do not rest on exterior things but on what we are living within ourselves.

4. MEDITATION CAN TRANSCEND DESIRE

The fourth noble truth on the path leading to the termination of suffering

"Just understanding, just thought, just word, just action, just mean of existence, just effort, just attention and just concentration."

Buddha

Meditation is a tool offering us the possibility not to be affected by our thought process anymore, and within the inner silence it allows us to become aware of the impermanence of material things and to understand that everything begins and ends. Therefore, everything that has a beginning will end sometime in the future. Everything that is unhappiness (pain, suffering) will end sometime in the future, everything that we deem happiness (joy) will also come to an end when its time comes. We will always lose in the future what we have acquired in the past whether it is wealth, a loved one, life, etc. And we will be sad (unhappy, suffering) according to the level of our desire to keep what we acquired. Suffering is based on the level of importance that we give to beings and things that we wish to acquire or that we wish to keep. Meditation allows us to realize that real happiness does not rest on material things, but within ourselves and our vision of the external world. The adage says that it is useless to conquer the world if one loses his soul while doing it.

Meditation is the research springboard of anyone wishing to better understand himself physically, mentally and spiritually with an objective to further understand life and creation in general.

It also allows us to better communicate and thus to better integrate ourselves into the universe in which we live.

Meditation is the element that allows us to transcend what we deem so solid and important in order to replace it with what is less consistent and nevertheless more important for the serenity of the human being.

Finally anyone practicing meditation will find inner happiness (harmony), the happiness that does not wither, the only stable happiness that will last indefinitely.

When we stop for a moment to analyze our life cycle, it becomes possible to grasp the order of every interlocking things around us. We must stop separating things composing our world; we should rather consider them as different parts of the same puzzle. Nothing is alien, nothing is really different, everything holds together, everything supports everything, and in fact everything is only various facets of a unique scene played at the theater of our dualist life.

We come to life to die, we forge unions that will come apart, we create children that will leave us, we are healthy and we will eventually get sick, we obtain wealth that we will lose, we are young and we will age. And nothing can change that, these are life guidelines and nothing can modify them. We all live at one moment or other these various ups and downs that will bring us suffering.

Life cycle

But we also live through these various life steps experiencing opposite emotions, that is to say that all these various steps will also bring us their lots of happiness that will wither away more or less rapidly to leave us stranded facing misery and suffering according to the level of our desire not to lose what we deem ours for always.

GRIEF (UNHAPPINESS)

> *"Confusion is the state of what is mixed, impossible to define."*
>
> *Golden rule of meditation*

CONFUSION

Confusion is another form of unhappiness or suffering. All human beings suffer from confusion at more or less elevated levels. One is confused when it becomes impossible to control the invasion of one's inner mental space by thousands of thoughts that seem to be coming from nowhere and everywhere.

All human beings are submitted to this intrusion starting at birth (and even before), and which continue as long as one is alive. And the level of confusion of a human being facing life depends on his capacity to isolate oneself from these thoughts and to process them according to their importance.

How many people are insomniacs because they cannot master the flux of these mental images attacking them, even more intensely during the night? A person who lets these thoughts invade their entire inner space, lives in total confusion. This state generates instability, insecurity, torments, pain, misunderstanding, disease, etc.

There is only one known mean to master this confusion and to experience harmony, calm, peace, serenity. One must set his attention on a sole point, object, sound, breathing, etc. while disregarding all other factors. This exercise is called meditation or the capacity to ignore the thought process.

The art of meditation allows one to disregard thought emergence and immersion and to concentrate on a sole attention point while disregarding all others. The practice of meditation generates the capacity to ignore the attack of the thoughts on the mental balance of one being and allows living harmoniously with the inner and outer aspects of our world.

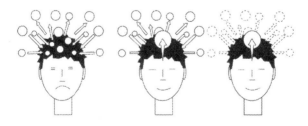

All human beings, those we normally call normal persons, us, are all more or less assailed by our thoughts and mental images, thus we are accordingly in a state of confusion. Let us consider this young man, above and to the left, assailed on all sides by these small white balls representing his thoughts. Some are emerging and others are immersing, meaning that they appear and disappear. We only have to close our eyes a moment while trying to keep our inner silence to experience a situation similar to this illustration. As soon as we give a little attention to our inner self, we realize this continuous invasion of our consciousness by thoughts that seem to come from nowhere. In fact these thoughts are generated by the bioelectrical work taking place within our brain. The bioelectrical energy inflow initiates cerebral reactions that generate the emergence and disappearance of images or thoughts. All our memories, all our experiences are stored within our neurons which, when activated, initiate more or less realistic images or thoughts. During the day, our brain has the capacity to interpret and to deliver to our consciousness more coherent images and thoughts, but at night, the same process is still going on and creates dreams that seem so unreal when we wake up in the morning. They are unreal because the coherent, analytical part of our brain is in a state of rest during sleep. Thus we visualise scenes that are often incredible but still, they are related to our current and past actions. During our wake-up periods the flux of thoughts is so intense that we identify with this assembly of thoughts emerging and immersing in our head. We identify to this thoughts assembly, we believe that we are this assembly of thoughts when in reality we are its essence. We are the thought source of everything existing in our world.

But let us return to the above illustration, the center character is also under an intense attack from his random thoughts but his attention is set on one point (that can be his breathing (prâna), an image, a location in his head, a word (mantra),

etc.) represented here by the arrow in front of a white circle bigger than the others. The inflow of thoughts is still present but its impact is a lot less important on the character. During meditation we set our attention on a point inside the head, the breathing process, a word or anything else but excluding anything else, without analysis, thus this object of concentration has priority and any other demand (thought) becomes secondary, thoughts are relegated in the background and with time we will be like the third character of the above illustration. His attention is so intense on his concentration point that he is capable to completely ignore the inflow of thoughts that still exist and carry on its dance.

In this state, peace takes the place of the endless dance of thoughts. In this state, one takes a step back regarding things of life that can trouble his inner harmony. In this state, one rests in a natural state and experiments an inner calm practically unknown to people in general, a state of consciousness and harmony unknown until then.

We just saw the three steps allowing passing from the state of confusion to one of harmony and control.

DESPAIR

> *"A person practicing meditation shows weakness when he allows their intellect to be obsessed with worldly thoughts."*
>
> *Golden rule of meditation*

When confusion becomes intolerable, one becomes obsessive; he then believes that he has no more control over his life and his environment.

Without control one is slaved to the endless thought process dictating its objectives. If these objectives are unreachable for this person, then confusion and despair set in.

Despair arises when one realizes that he has no more power over his environment or no longer has the capacity to modify the course of his life and soon the emotional charge is so heavy that he cannot foresee the possibility to intervene to change his own condition. The person is so beclouded by this emotional charge that he believes it is impossible to take action to solve his problems. According to him, based on his understanding of the situation, there is no more solution, the person is backed against the wall of life.

In the impossibility to act on his exterior world, in the impossibility to change, modify what goes wrong, he has only his body left and in a final gesture he takes action against this last thing that he is still capable to alter. Suicide is in fact the last gesture, the last action that one believes he is able to accomplish. A person in deep despair, believing that he is incapable of destroying the source of suffering, destroys the sufferer in a last attempt to cancel suffering.

During meditation, when one sets his attention on something other than his problems, the emotional charge is automatically reduced, thus also confusion, this permits to take required actions to return to a harmonious state. Meditation is a time-out period, a moment of mental rest in our everyday highly active life. It

allows one to take a step back and gives him the ability not to let himself be submerged by the worries that life tirelessly showers us with. Therefore a person practicing meditation can see and analyse problems more clearly and thus take appropriate actions to resolve them.

NATURE OF THE HUMAN BEING

THE EVOLUTION OF THE HUMAN BEING

> *"Human being is the sole animal who seems to have the faculty to acknowledge his spiritual nature."*
>
> *Paramahansa the Kagyütpa*

Energy is the basic element constituting all matters including living beings, thus human beings. Great physicians state that when they fragment the atom and its elements there comes a time during which matter-energy behaves like thought. That one moment the elements are there and then they suddenly disappear and they seem to exist or to take on a polarity only in the presence of an observer. Would quantic physics rest on the thought of those observing it?

The atom's components, constituting all matter would be thought, matter itself would be thought and finally living beings would also be thought, including humans. Here is an interesting theory and that could explain many of life's mysteries. Among others, it become possible to name various evolutionary steps leading to human beings which could be: thought, energy, atom, dust, inert matter (planets), living matter like vegetable and animal including man who in time realizes his place within the great cosmic machine and progressively returns to the primary essence, thought. The loop is then closed; human being is vibrating from moment to moment to a higher octave within the great symphony of the primordial thought and creation.

Human being in his entirety does not seem to evolve or change with time. This vision is due to the fact that we are all stopped in time. For us a few decades or centuries represent eternities that at the universal level are only momentary fluctuations of space-time. A few seconds at the universe level transform into millennium for us humble humans.

Thus the mass of beings to our eyes does not seem to evolve if we look to the past and attempt to see the evolving difference between man of today and man of 2000 years ago for example. No significant changes, men were killing each other then and they are still doing it today. Men were destroying their environment with the means at their disposal at the time and are doing the same today with their current means. Therefore, man has not really changed except for his technical and material evolution, but within we find no significant improvement.

But at the individual level, each one of us can change; we can transform, analyse, understand, change behaviour and learn what is secret and inaccessible to most people on this planet living with the overwhelming noise of the thought process that, in the absence of control, generates confusion and suffering.

Everything starts with self-questioning. In the absence of self-questioning, questing, there can be no change, no modification nor transformation of the human being. If one believes that he knows everything, if he believes that he possesses the truth, it is impossible for him to learn something new, to quest oneself and his environment. But if one questions his behaviour and his knowledge then it becomes possible for this individual to evolve and understand one's life beyond general human understanding.

When there is questioning, soul-searching, there is a possibility to quickly grasp the essence of human beings and the environment in which they live.

We are all very critical of others' actions and decisions but very tolerant and understanding of our own. We are experts in rationalizing our own behaviours. Next time you criticize someone, at the end of your comment add the following expression to your statement: "yes, but me, what I would have done differently in his place?" and answer this simple question sincerely. Your attempt to answer this question will help you see the point of view of the person that you were criticizing a few minutes ago. There is a lot to learn from this simple method of questioning oneself.

THE BODY

"Our body being illusion and transitory, it is useless to give it too much importance."

Golden rule of meditation

The atomic components that we discussed above are grouped into genetic aggregates constituting the human body as well as any other form of life; they have migrated from one being to another through procreation since the birth of our planet. We are the result of an infinite chain of evolution. We retained some characteristics of our submarine ancestors of several million years ago while we rejected others, and these are the factors that make us what we biologically are today as human beings, we represent the result of the genetic mix of our fathers and mothers, who were both individually transporting their respective fathers' and mothers' genes and we could go back like this to the dawn of life on the earth and beyond. All terrestrial life is based on the same genetic foundation; we are all coming from the same root. Human beings are all physically different while being all similar due to their genetic legacy.

The biological aggregate assemblies forming any being determine these physical characteristic variations. In our modern time of human and various animal species genome sequencing and genetic research allowing us to become aware of the pathological trend of beings through gene sequencing and analysis of targeted population, we have no choice but to acknowledge our common root. It is not possible to ignore what we really are anymore.

We are made of assemblies of assemblies of various genes gathered over the thousands of years of our existence on this world. All those tendencies, genetic or others, are forming the human body and influence our mental or intellectual aggregates integrated into what we call the human being.

THE MIND

> *"Being different from the multitude in thoughts and actions is the sign of a superior being."*
>
> *Golden rule of meditation*

If the body including the brain is composed of genetic aggregates, the mental, this intellectual part of our being, is nothing else than the interrelation work of various components of the biological brain, the latter is only the intellectual legacy of a being made of various aggregates taking root in the analysis that the brain makes of different stimuli experienced during each moment of its existence. The intellectual (mental) baggage of a human being, self-awareness, take its source in the brain, which is simply an analytical machine equipped with a data base (capacity to memorize and store data) that of course makes our most modern computer look like a toy. The brain receives messages from various sensors (eyes, ears, nose, fingers, tongue, skin, etc.), analyses and classifies them by order of importance regarding the survival and wellbeing of the carrier being as a whole. The human being keeps a genetic memory from his parents. This mental baggage also includes all practical and theoretical knowledge of a person, including those acquired during conversations and all social or other reports forming the life of a human being.

The French logic engineer Jean-Louis Krivine just launched an advanced theory addressed to our contemporary scientific community. He states that the brain is only a big calculating machine and the computers that we are currently trying to develop with more and more powerful processing capacities are in fact only attempts to copy our own brain. He also states that the Lambda language, a calculation process invented during the 1930s, is similar to that of our brain.

The mental legacy of human as a whole is all experiences, analyses and synthesis processed during the course of one's existence. The conscious and unconscious brain stores all that a being has experienced since the beginning of pregnancy in the mother's womb.

Each gene also carries a genetic legacy not to call it a mental legacy, and since the beginning of time they influence today's beings. Scientists increasingly accept the theory that each gene, each molecule, etc., possesses a form of intelligence. We all know that after only a few days following procreation, the few molecules forming the small being in the making carry a very evolved program allowing them to differentiate when the time comes to form various parts and organs of the body. This molecular assembly has the capacity to decide the formation of one organ or another according to a pre-established genetic program. This is what allows human beings, for example, to have two eyes, two legs, two arms, etc. etc. It would be very strange to live in a world not conforming to the basic recipe contained into the genetic legacy of its population.

The brain, this super biological machine allows us to take informed decisions regarding everything that we experience during our life. These decisions are based on the analysis performed by the brain; this analysis is based on the comparison between some similar or more or less comparable facts related to the decision to be taken.

As a whole, the human is composed of the sum of all its genetic, biological, mental and intellectual elements. We cannot subtract one of these elements without practically destroying the whole.

Beyond analysis and comparison, the human being is enslaved to his aggregates or appetites, whether biological such as sex, hunger, thirst, warmth, cold, etc., or mental, psychological such as the need for love, possession, gain, happiness, without taking into account the needs generated by mental blocks or psychological engrams acquired during one's life. Mental or psychological blocks or engrams, the results of old extreme frustrations or suffering, sometimes leads humans to actions that do not comply with the social consensus in which we live.

THE AGGREGATES

> *"One practicing meditation must know that all visible phenomena are illusory and unreal."*
>
> *Golden rule of meditation*

Aggregates are biological assemblies for the body, and intellectual assemblies for the mental, constituting the human being. These assemblies are active entities meeting other assemblies to create new ones indefinitely. No aggregate, whether biological or intellectual, is permanent. Human beings like everything existing in the universe are composed of temporary assemblies of different assemblies of various assemblies that are mutating, transforming constantly.

We are beings in continuous biological and intellectual mutation contemplating a universe in perpetual transformation. Nothing is stable, nothing is static, everything is moving, everything is transforming and from one moment to another we are the spectators of our world's renewal, of a new universe.

The human being must adapt and survive within this turbulent instability, in a universe where structures become increasingly complex, more and more difficult to grasp and manage.

THE DOMINANT AGGREGATES

> *"A person practicing meditation must acquire the practical wisdom of the path by walking it."*
>
> *Golden rule of meditation*

In order to survive in a world in continuous mutation, humans have developed survival strategies allowing various aspects of their being to take on the management of body operations according to the competence of these respective aspects (aggregates).

Various biological or intellectual element assemblies dominating the brain are also named dominant aggregates. As all other aggregates, the latters are also in perpetual mutation, continuous modification. Their transformation is maintained by the interactions between themselves and with those coming from the exterior, from our own actions and interactions with the world. At each moment in our life, a dominating thought (an aggregate of several thought elements) takes charge of the human being's brain and determines the action that the body will take. At all times this dominant aggregate must fight to keep its dominance and pursue its objective. Let us take a simple example: imagine that you are comfortably sitting and reading a book, suddenly you feel some hunger (the biological aggregate takes charge of the brain by dislodging the current dominating aggregate, this new dominating aggregate orders your body to rise and go to the refrigerator), on your way someone anticipating your action intercepts you and tells you that if you want to lose some weight you should not carry on your project of eating something at this time. Following this statement the intellectual aggregate, realizing the importance to remain slim, takes back control of your brain, suppresses the biological aggregate and orders the body to go back, sit and continue reading while rationalizing that eating at this time can only cause an unhealthy weight gain, etc. This example is maybe overly simple but it shows what is happening when a person takes a decision, most of the time more or less consciously, to do one thing rather than another. This overall process takes place more or less consciously and at all times you are convinced that you (yourself) are taking the decisions while in fact the aggregates within you are controlling your brain and body according to the situations and needs. They attend our own existence taking place outside of the ultimate ME, this spark of consciousness not composed of aggregates but only of a sole non analytical being.

We believe that we are continuously in control of our body, but no one can deny that one's behaviour varies according to the situations we face. Take notice of your behaviour during a face to face conversation with a man and of your behaviour during the same situation facing a woman. It is then easy to observe that we are almost never the same person from one moment of our life to another. We differ according to events, we adapt to different situations. And we believe that the one adapting to events is the ME while different parts of us (the aggregates) are in fact taking over and taking action in our place.

We identify with our aggregates. Most people believe that they are their aggregate assemblies (thoughts) and that if they were to set them aside, they would not exist anymore.

They do not realize that in reality they are only a spark of consciousness floating on the ocean of illusions.

THE MIND

"The greatest happiness is to possess inner peace."

The elegant thoughts

The spirit or the REAL ME is this presence inhabiting each one of us. This entity does not think, does not analyse, does not act, it only observes. It is the cause of every one of our existences. It is made of emptiness or void and cannot be affected by the material world that in fact is emanating from it and in which we are all live. The only characteristic of the ultimate reality is to BE.

It seems that most of us do not know that we are a spirit and furthermore that we practically never acknowledge our inner makeup or realized the presence of this being representing the infinity of the universe, who in fact is ourselves. We are spirit, we live in an ocean of nothingness but we are the spiritual, intellectual and material causes and effects of the world's existence.

We do not know who we really are because we are immersed in this mass of aggregates (thought assemblies) and totally subjugated by our senses making us believe that only matter or sensations exist.

Yet it is quite easy to communicate with this entity, we need only to experience the inner silence, to subdue our thought process for a while to realize that within silence (during meditation when the thought process no longer affects us) resides a presence and that this presence is none other than the REAL ME. The REAL ME resides in all living beings of the universe. All other parts of us, body, brain, thoughts, personality, taste, sex, etc. are only illusory characteristics that we use to act upon the surrounding material world. This is what most of us believe to be!

In order to realize that we initially are a spirit we need to become aware that we still exist, even when we are isolated from our thought process. Most people assume that they will not exist anymore if they ignore their thoughts. That consciousness is nothing else than the overall thought assembly, the accumulation of all thoughts passing through our mind, nothing is more false. It is only within our inner emptiness that we can possibly contemplate our real nature.

The art of meditation allows us to visit, study and taste this inner space and to acknowledge the essence of our REAL ME. From this contact we will emerge calmer, wiser, happier and more harmonious, finally less bound to the things of this world without necessarily rejecting them.

LAWS

THE LAW OF ACTION/REACTION

> *"The best practice is to live in perfect compliance with the law of action/reaction."*
>
> *Golden rule of meditation*

The only law existing in the universe is the law of action/reaction, you will argue that there are also the laws of nature and the laws set in place by men, but I would answer that these laws are illusory and are not taken into account within creation, but by us all within our natural, personal and social environments. The laws of nature are those that rest on the law of action/reaction in the world that we know. As for us humans, we invented laws that are in fact consensus of society allowing us to live together in harmony.

But when we are talking about the universal law, the law that does not need a police force to enforce it, we are talking about the law of action/reaction and none other, and this law is managing creation as a whole. The universe does not assume emotions or moral, it does not take into account what we identify as good or bad. Good and bad do not exist in the universe beside the human being's perception who owns this notion of the bipolarity of his environment. Everything perceived by a human being is part of the bipolar world in which he is immersed. He is continuously balancing between what he sees as white and what he sees as black, between what he believes to be good or bad.

Man lives in a world of perception, identification and classification. Nothing can be done about this, our internal program is set that way and we are all slaved to it, it is almost impossible for us to escape from it. First we become aware of something, a sound, an object, an animal or a person. We automatically try to identify it, this is done by bipolar comparison, if it is a person we will identify it as a male or female, young or old, nice looking or not, clean or neglected, known or unknown, friend or foe, etc. Finally we will file this analysis in our mental data base, for example, this is a young man, he is my nephew, he looks like my sister, and he is friendly. Based on the results obtained we will then take action, in this case talk to him for example. And, if this person is a stranger, with a sinister look and if he starts yelling, we could identify him as dangerous, which would trigger a glandular and mental process that would prompt us to take some actions in order to protect our own physical integrity. We could decide to attack him or to run away, according that our feelings and the kind of a person we are, our constitution, age, sex, etc.

Everything surrounding us is subjected to this program (consciously or not) before taking any action, a complete process of evaluation and measure takes place that reaches a verdict, from which will follow the action that we will take. Of course, this analysis and decision-making process takes place in a few fractions of a second and often partially consciously or completely unconsciously.

The perceived universe rests on bipolarity. Without this duality, what we call creation could not be perceived as we do now with the various sensors available to us, such as eyes, ears, nose, fingers, skin, etc. Everything is based on positive and negative, everything has its opposite, white and black, good and bad, male and female, high and low, left and right, etc., and this list is far from being exhaustive.

Our emotions are also subjected to bipolarity, for example love has its opposite, hate, joy, sadness, happiness, suffering, etc. This is the reason that makes us invent all kinds of laws that are structured around this bipolar notion of good and bad. By social consensus, we establish society's rules allowing us to live in harmony within a community. The rules are not necessarily the same for every societies since they are based on a social consensus with notions of good and bad that may differ from one to another. What people believe to be bad in North America could be seen as good somewhere else in the world. The laws and regulations in China or in Iran for example, are quite different from those in America. This does not means that foreign laws are better or worse than ours; this only shows that the social consensus is different.

For the universe, our laws and regulations have no importance, only action/reaction is taken into account. This action/reaction law manages all including us.

PROCESS OF THE UNIVERSAL LAW

> *"The universal law ensures that each action generates a result and produces a reaction."*
>
> Paramahansa the Kagyütpa

Any action generates a reaction, affecting stars, planets and living beings and even inert matter. The reaction can be felt more intensely the closer it gets to the action. Therefore, if the action is taken in your home, the reaction will be felt more intensely in your immediate environment. The effect of reaction will diminish as the distance between you and the action increases. It is like a stone thrown in a pond, the rock falls in the water and creates circles that become larger and larger as they get farther away from the impact center. As the circles grow larger, waves become smaller, the impact of the rock becomes less.

A wise man once said that a grain of sand cannot be moved on earth without affecting the whole universe. Each thing has its place, everything reacts with all, and nothing is perfectly isolated from the rest of the universe. It is like imagining a huge sphere so full of balls that it would be impossible to move one without moving all others. This is the type of universe in which we are living, space separating us is only illusion, and this is only what we perceive. At the energy level the universe is a great basin filed at full capacity where everything exists in contingency with everything and everything is germane to everything. We may wish to be alone, we may think that we are alone and isolated from the rest of the world but this is only wishful dreaming and a false perception, we are all linked to one another at the energy level. And one's actions automatically affect others.

Everything that we perceive is part of the bipolar shamble, and we attempt to adapt, to survive in this ocean of confusion. We like this and dislike that, we believe this to be good and that to be bad without any other reasons than the dictatorship of our culture and perception of the world. We navigate on this sea of illusions that are our extremes and all the gray zones between them.

Based on this very precious data, acknowledging the existence of the action/reaction law, one can take control of his own life and do what he wants with it. If I meet someone, insult him and beat him, there are good chances that he will wish to do the same to me. If one acts with warmth and friendliness toward someone he will probably become a good friend. Everything is based on this premise; my actions are the cause of the reactions that will affect me at one time or another. If I dream to reach an objective and take actions to reach it, there are good chances that my dream will come true. This is not new, but we so often forget it that it is good to repeat it once in a while to remember the fact of life in this world. The "New Testament" was already telling us that thousands of years ago "one living by the sword will die by the sword", this is only another way to state that our actions are affecting our future. In fact, our future is the result of our past and current actions. We use our current actions to create our future, thus it is very important to take into consideration what we are and do today and we will have a very accurate view of what we will be tomorrow.

Let us use the present to launch actions that will create a good future where we will be at peace and harmonious with our self and others. Let us do today what we will be proud of tomorrow.

BENEFITS OF MEDITATION

> *"One is doing oneself good be reducing his attachment to visible things that are transitory and unreal and by experimenting reality."*
>
> *Golden rule of meditation*

PHYSICAL BENEFITS

We could write hundreds of pages on the benefits that meditation can bring to one applying oneself industriously to it. But we will only analyse here what is meditation per se and what this or those states can produce as results.

Meditation is a deep state of attention and calm that automatically produces a beneficial mind and body relaxation. It is well known that targeting one's attention and relaxation will lower the metabolism and immediately reduce the level of stress. Lowering the level of stress, anxiety and tension, slows down the respiratory and cardiac rhythms, which gives both organs a resting moment that they need to restore their strength and energy to carry on their work efficiently.

Modern medicine tells us that most diseases affecting us are due in great part to the state of stress in which our world is immersing us. Stress has the property to undermine our energy and to weaken our immune system, with the result that we become more vulnerable to diseases. Thus meditation is an excellent discipline to reduce this state which makes us prone to a life in poor health.

Relaxation, intellectual and physical rest, better attention capacity, acknowledgment of reality, detachment from material things, acknowledgment of illusion, simplification of world issues, reduction of the emotional level, greater self-confidence, certainty, harmony, happiness, etc. These are some of the benefits that the practice of meditation can generate.

Attention: Meditation is not a medical treatment. Meditation is a discipline permitting to improve our health, by giving the body in general and the immune system in particular the capacity to do their work of prevention and protection against health issues.

MENTAL BENEFITS

> *"For a person of superior intelligence, the best meditation is to remain in a state of quiescence."*
>
> *Golden rule of meditation*

Viewed differently, beyond the benefits of relaxation and of its physical influence, meditation by allowing us to reduce our attachment to our life issues, makes us more patient and more tolerant of others thus gives us the possibility to live in a more harmonious and less stressing environment. Furthermore, it gives us the capacity to better understand others and life in general, making us see the world from a more optimistic angle.

The practice of deep concentration (meditation) generates an improved level of attention for things in life, whether at work or at home. Memory is the first faculty that the practice of meditation will improve. A better memory, a greater self-confidence and a better control of one's emotions, these improvements allow one practicing meditation to lead a better life within oneself and with others.

Attention: Meditation is not a psychological treatment. Meditation is a discipline allowing us to improve almost all aspects of our intelligence, thus our personal and social life. Meditation is a life practice allowing us to take advantage of a new vision of ourselves and the world.

SPIRITUAL BENEFITS

> *"Think with all your body"*
>
> *Taisen Deshimaru*

Meditation will generate several physical and mental benefits but in the end it will make one much less affected by emotions and a lot less enslaved to things of this world. When a person feels detached from what most of us are accepting as most important, it then becomes easy to be less affected by it, which frees us from its capacity to enslave us. We are attached (slaved) only to what we give importance to. We are free from all that we deem negligible, without importance. I believe that we should understand what this implies. Synthesis: If I give importance to something, it automatically becomes important to me and therefore will affect my life accordingly, the reverse will produce the opposite. Thus it is better to be neutral, or at least not attached or enslaved to what others and I personally may deem important. The result is that I am partially free of at least those things.

Meditation allows one to experiment more or less detachment from the material world according to the purity of the meditation state. I should rather say that it allows one to see the material world from another perspective; it allows one to observe the world without being necessarily immersed in it. Material detachment is followed by an awakening of the consciousness. Consciousness awakening brings about the opportunity to see and evaluate our surrounding world, to deliver us from the egocentric ego (aggregate assemblies) and to allow us to see that some other beings exist outside of us who have as much importance as we do within the greater scheme of the universe. This awakening prompts us to understand that we do not have much importance within the greater scheme of life but that we have our space either more or less important than that of others. Specifically, it makes us realize that other individual worlds exist outside of our own and outside each of us. Egocentrism is over, since it becomes clear that the world is turning not around OURSELF but around the interpretation that we make of the world in which we live.

Then comes the acknowledgment of illusion, what we consider our reality, which is in fact only unreality and illusion. This illusory reality only rests on our means to perceive it, on our sensors. What is real for you is not necessarily real for me in most cases and vice versa. The reality of a Chinese person is not necessarily the same as mine, etc. It is possible to realize the absence of reality of our world by observing that it is constantly changing, always mutating, transforming and so on, nothing is stable.

Reality with a big "R" must be stable and unchanged from one moment to the next if we want to depend on it, is it not? Finally, this is what must be reality to me, it must be what we could call a stable data, and this permanent, unchangeable reality is impossible to be found in the outside world. Everything around us is changing, is altered by wear and tear, becomes something else, everything surrounding us is unstable and transitory, in permanent mutation as we have seen earlier.

One practicing meditation discovers the only thing in our world that always remains the same, and this thing is the SILENCE found during meditation. This silence is the same as the one experienced by the greatest wise masters of the world since this silence does not change. Within silence rests emptiness and this void also never changes, it cannot be altered. It is impossible to find something else than silence in our material world that is immutable, unchanged and unchangeable. I am inviting you to inform me about anything else that you could find with this characteristic of non-mutability, non-transformation. Silence is the only real thing that we know because it is immutable and permanent contrary to anything else.

Therefore, it is possible to acknowledge the illusion; it implies the erroneous interpretation of data or facts of our surrounding world. Illusion is anything that changes, mutates or is transformed because of time or any other factors. If something changes, it means that it is unstable and cannot last in time, thus it is impermanent and illusory. Meditation allows us to recognise what is stable, without movement, without transformation and also what is transitory, changeable, and transformable. Anyone practicing meditation knows for a fact that what is unstable is in fact unreal, illusory and what is stable, empty, devoid of anything is the sole reality, the only thing on which it is possible to depend now and in the future. Furthermore in meditation we call this emptiness, void, the Refuge, a place where it is always possible to find a refuge in total security. The Refuge is a space without borders where nothing and nobody can find you, attack you, touch you, alter you, this is a place of perfect safety and serenity. This is this place where it is always possible to fall back to set aside what is bordering us, what can harm us, where even our thoughts cannot affect us anymore.

The capacity to be able to experiment, to taste total immobility for a few moments will offer you more benefits than long vacations in the South or elsewhere. A wise man of times past was saying to his adepts: "a second of inner silence has more value than a thousand years of ceaseless mental turbulences and noises".

When someone becomes familiar with meditation, these more or less long moments of silence become moments of great calm, serenity and sometimes one may experience an illumination. These instants of consciousness give us the opportunity to have a glimpse of the universe's reality, the ultimate truth. These moments of intense delight only last the time during which we are becoming conscious of it, since as soon as the analytical system residing in each of us takes charge of this experience, it transports it into our bipolar world where begin the assessment and analysis that will make it into another event devoid of reality, because it will then have been compared, analysed, classified, etc.

Therefore, it is practically impossible to really realize, based on our bipolar standards of realization, that we just experienced an illumination, which is a moment of universal truth not rooted in our illusory and random world. This instant of awareness only lasts the time of its realization, just before to the brain starts dissecting it in order to make sense of it and to file it with millions of other experiences of our daily life. It will have become bipolar, thus impermanent and illusory. Only the memory remains of this instant of illumination and clairvoyance, but such precious moments allow us to see the everyday world with more serenity and tolerance.

During meditation, following these instants of awareness the ultimate realization may come. This state of awareness locates us in the universe; it places us where we are supposed to be. It identifies us in all our importance or in all our insignificance as being part of the greater universal machine. The smallest grain of sand has its importance in the universe, thus it is easy to understand that each human being has also its place in it. The human being is in the universe an indispensable element through all his components and all his experiences.

Since this state is impossible to reproduce in a so-called "normal" state, it is interesting to imagine the importance that each one of us can have in the process of the great cosmic adventure.

Meditation reveals that each one of us incorporates all the data of the universe, as our ADN contains all the data to create a human being. We are all and we are nothing, we are nothing and we are all.

This is what it is possible to glimpse and experience through meditation at the spiritual level. But at the material level these instants of awareness, these experiences beyond what is called reality provide a wider vision of life to the meditator, this allows one to live in harmony with the surrounding world and with the universe as a whole.

Then comes the time during deep meditation to acknowledge that everything is harmony in the universe, that everything is in perfect equilibrium and that if it were not the case, the universe would be different and would fix this anomaly. Then it becomes easy to see the world with serenity, to become more carefree for our greater good.

It becomes possible to put our emotions in the background and to see the world as it is doing what it has to do, to realize that our world is in a constant state of creation and destruction (uncreation). Emotions only serve to give importance to the illusory things of our world and to make us unhappy.

One must be looking for silence in order to find real happiness.

MEDITATION DOES NOT ISOLATE ONE FROM NORMAL LIFE

> *"Life is nothing but a long meditation period. Anyone aware of what he is doing at the time of doing it without thinking about anything else meditates."*
>
> *Golden rule of meditation*

People often think that the practice of meditation isolates from the tangible world in which we all live. It is quite the opposite in fact, the practice of this discipline encourages us to take control of our own life and of what we really want to become. It is not a religion or a sect of any kind, meditation is a discipline and a personal endeavour happening within each one of us and one must never let anyone else interfere with this proceeding. Moreover, it is very important to question everything written in this book or any other book that you may read, until you have validated all those statements by yourself through meditation at your own pace and own way. Only your own personal meditation experience will allow you to assimilate your own truth and not that of someone else.

Meditation is an individual experience allowing to discover one's own truth, one's own path leading to happiness and salvation.

Meditation is a discipline that must be completely integrated in our everyday life. It is possible to meditate, to keep mental silence, while walking, playing, working, etc. and to meditate one has to simply keep inner silence, to ignore the thought process, "be present". To meditate is to experience silence in one's head, nothing else, whatever method of meditation one is practicing to reach this state. To meditate is to live the present moment, "NOW".

MEDITATION IN LIFE

> *"Always keep an alert consciousness while walking, speaking, eating, etc."*
>
> *Golden rule of meditation*

The art of meditation is nothing like a gymnastic regiment or any other discipline that takes a few moments of your day. With practice, the art of meditation will become part of your life. This is not some kind of part-time activity added to one's daily life. Meditation must become an integral part of one's life and of what one's really is. Meditation must be present at each moment of the day and night, there is no time off. The art of meditation is an element that one integrates into daily life, therefore each action taken and even each word spoken are influenced by this new way of life. This means that meditation will become an element that will influence every moment of your life. Meditation is a state through which one's entire life is filtered.

When I walk on a sidewalk or on the trail with my dogs, I meditate by concentrating on my breathing and by being aware of my entire being walking, but still during this period it is possible to admire and taste nature's beauty without analysis. It is important to become the OBSERVER. Meditation is also the realization of the body moving through space and time, without analysis. Acknowledgement without analysis of what is happening within us and around us is meditation. The main hurdle is the analysis process that since all times uses the dualistic factors in the evaluation and classification of one's every moment in life. One must not analyse, evaluate, compare or think, one must only observe, as an infant observes those marvelous light reflections that his eyes are transmitting to him and this without the need to understand the source or the essence of those beautiful colours. One must see without trying to understand. ONE MUST TASTE without the desire to know the recipe.

Finally, the overall meditation process rests on the awareness of what one is doing at each instant of his life. If we are not conscious of what we are doing at each instant, then WE DO NOT EXIST! Thus, it is very important to be aware that we are breathing, speaking, eating, etc . . . The only moment having some importance is the present, the NOW. This is the sole moment on which one can have some impact. This is the sole moment allowing us to act upon our future. This is the only tool given to us to build what we wish our future to be. The past is behind us and cannot be modified, the future is the extension of the current moment, thus NOW is the only place (moment) during which one must live if one wishes to take advantage of life. One living in the past can only experience disappointment and one living only in the future without doing anything in the present to shape it to his will is only feeding on disillusions. The only moment of importance is now, right now. Yesterday is gone and tomorrow is not there yet; the time to take advantage of is NOW.

Meditation is a mindset and principle of life. To sit and meditate is good, but we can meditate while doing anything else, any actions of our current life. It is important to only eat when eating, to only cut the grass when cutting the grass and to do only one task at a time while at the office if one is at work or anywhere else. When one concentrates fully on one's actions, there is no goal to reach but to do well what one is doing. We do not ask ourselves if we will earn a lot of money doing what we are doing, or if we will finally complete the mowing of the grass in one hour instead of two or whether we will obtain a management position or the salary increase we so desired. We do what we do fully in the now without questioning ourselves.

While working this way we do not waste energy wondering about this or that in the past or the future. On the contrary, we use our work as a mean to remain present, to improve our attention capacity, our level of efficiency as well as the quality of our product, and this, and not the questioning, will bring us closer to what we wish to become..

When working while being present (that is while meditating), fatigue does not affect us, quite the contrary we store energy and we take advantage of a state of beneficial inner peace. Goodbye stress, welcome calm, harmony, welcome energy and power, all this added to the pleasure to do well what one wishes to do now.

TECHNIQUES

THE TECHNIQUES OF MEDITATION

> *"Meditation is not a mean to reach a goal, but rather both; it is a mean and goal at the same time."*
>
> *Krishnamurti*

Meditation techniques are numerous and one is certainly as good as any other. Some teachings request to set one's attention on a "mantra" tirelessly repeating a series of words, or on a sound, a point, also on silence, emptiness, void, love, etc. and I am sure I forget some of them. We will only expand on a few of those meditation techniques or teachings. But one must understand that a mantra, breathing, sound or any other concentration means are only tools used to set one's attention on only one thing without analysis. Therefore they are only means to reach a state of mind and nothing else.

I travelled the world for decades looking for the best meditation method, the one best suited to me; I was initiated to several meditation methods, which finally did not meet what I was looking for. After practicing them for a while, I would find them complicated, tainted with various ceremonies that had nothing to do with meditation proper. Not satisfied with my findings, I launched a search for the simplest method of meditation known to this day.

This adventure took me to the confines of Nepal, travelling through India's major cities, namely Mumbai, Benares, Bangalore, and several others.

At the end of this search I discovered MahaMudra, the Great Symbol by excellence. The wise man Tilopa was saying about this method, "One needs only not to imagine, not to think, not to analyse, not to reflect, but only to keep one's mind in its natural and free state."

This discipline does not include any doctrine or ceremonials. Everything is happening within you and with you. You shall not give any credibility to any verbal or written statements, you must experiment through silence in order to verify statements from others and understand according to your own personality. No one should attempt to force you to do this or that.

But we also have to realize that we are living in countries immersed in very different cultures from the one that developed this discipline. While analysing these different methods of concentration of the attention we can determine what is really important and what is accessory, especially when we are well aware that the sole important point is to set one's attention on only one thing without analysis, to remain alert and aware to finally reach inner silence.

RELAXATION BREATHING

> *"Breathing is the mirror of your state of mind."*
>
> *Meditation precept*

Before starting any meditation session it is recommended to do some breathing exercises in order to bring a deep state of calm to the body and mind and especially to eliminate stress and tension gathered during your recent activities.

One needs only to breath deeply ten (10) times while focussing the attention on the air movement through the body. Take a long inhale by the nose and follow its path through the throat and down to fill the lower part of the lungs until you can feel your belly push a little outward, then the air continues to fill the median and upper parts of the lungs. While exhaling the air goes out of the upper, median and lower lungs until the diaphragm pulls the belly a little inward. Then repeat the same process ten times.

Breathe slowly without precipitation and exhale the same way smoothly. The air slides easily one way and the other. Do not force anything when inhaling or exhaling. Do not make a significant pause between inhalations and exhalations, let the breath takes its own rhythm without conditioning it, let the air in and the air out of your lungs.

After completing ten deep respirations, go back to a normal breathing and take a moment to look within yourself and you will feel a state of calm invade your whole body and mind. Take advantage of this moment to ensure that all tension has left all parts of your body and that you are ready to meditate.

ACTUAL MEDITATION STEPS

REFUGE AND COMMITMENT

"Balance, relaxation and natural"

Lama Kong Ka

No one can go anywhere before identifying the destination, selecting an itinerary, or accomplish anything without establishing an execution schedule. It is no different with meditation.

If your objective is to better know yourself, to have a better knowledge of the world, to learn where you are coming from or where you are going, if you acknowledge that it is possible to reduce the pain and suffering that life brings to you, to lower your level of stress or fatigue or to increase your energy level, if you realize that you have to make some efforts to obtain something, to acquire a discipline, then I recommend that you continue reading this book and to gather the information that you need to learn how to meditate and reach your goal.

The first thing needed is to set an objective and then not to be distracted from this decision and to persist in practicing the discipline of attention concentration.

The state of meditation is a refuge, you will discover this place within you where no one can touch you, reach you, influence you, attack you or alter you in any way. This is a place where calm, peace, void and absence of thought reside. This is the only place where even you cannot intervene. You can only find refuge there and observe. This is the inner space where there is no analysis, no attempt to identify; this is this place where you dwell as an observer exclusive of everything else. From this place you will come back as a child amazed and delighted after only observing, without any form of analysis or understanding. This is also a source of infinite energy that is yours if you know how to take ownership of this additional gift. And it is in this state of silence and harmony that the ultimate truth will unveil itself to you.

One must start meditating for short periods, smoothly, without rigidity. But with persistence you will break one by one all the barriers that are trying to close the passage for anyone attempting to destroy the wall of illusion and see face to face the reason behind what we see and experiment in this dualistic world.

BODY POSITIONS AND SUITABLE ENVIRONMENT

> *"There can be no mental discipline without body discipline."*
>
> *Golden rule of meditation*

The beginner usually asks when and where to meditate. As we have just seen above, there is no particular moment or place to meditate, quite the contrary, one must give it priority anywhere at all times.

But we need to understand that meditation cannot instantly become a discipline integrated into one's whole life. Thus one has to accustom body and mind to a new way of life. At the beginning, it is recommended to meditate in the morning just out of bed or at night just before going to bed. In fact, you have to find a moment during the day when you are calm, with few risks of being disturbed. It is preferable to always use the same place, especially at the beginning, so the body and mind will not have to continuously readapt to a new environment. The fact of always meditating in the same place at the same time of the day acts as a signal to the mind indicating that it is time to meditate. Meditation is better practiced on an empty stomach, thus ensure that your digestion does not distract you during your sessions. The duration of a session should not be too long at the start of your practice. In the beginning a few minutes (10 minutes) will be enough to bring the calm, relaxation and energy you are looking for and to acknowledge that it is possible to establish short periods of silence in your head. To attain inner silence, even in a partial fashion, is a great achievement. To live an instant of silence is better than a million years of distraction. With time, you will be able to extend your meditation periods according to your capacity of concentration. Do not be discouraged, you must persevere and slowly you will achieve all the progress that you projected and are anticipating.

The oriental meditation masters often recommend body postures that are more or less foreign to our culture. Indians sit in lotus and tailor positions because these are the way they have been sitting for thousands of years. I do not recommend to American or European people to conform to these body postures since they are foreign and often uncomfortable for us. Discomfort has a negative impact on meditation as are any nonchalant body postures by the way.

But if your body flexibility allows it, the tailor sitting position is excellent for meditation because the body is in balance; this position prompts the mind to remain more alert.

SITTING POSITION

> *"Sitting in a quiet place, without moving, in a good position and without saying a word, mind empty of any good or bad thoughts."*
>
> *Taisen Deshimaru*

For a successful meditation one is looking for a good comfortable position that will not create cramps or uneasiness for the duration of the session. However, it is recommended to keep the back straight and not resting on the back of the seat in order to avoid drowsiness. When the back is not resting on anything, it would seem that the brain remains more on guard to keep the body in balance, this is done unconsciously and the mind remains alert. Thus, the back must remain straight and not resting on anything if possible and it is recommended to cross the feet under the seat in order for the bottom and thighs to rest well on the seat, the hands will rest one on top of the other on the thighs just below the belly, this posture will allow you to remain in the meditation position for long periods when you will feel confident that you are able to do it.

It is also possible to meditate in other positions.

WHILE WALKING

> *"All of a sudden while walking, I stopped, suddenly realizing that I had no more body. All I could see was this bright immensity, omnipresent, perfect, lucid and serene."*
>
> *Han Shan*

Walking is ideal for meditation, it is possible to walk while synchronising one's breathing with each steps. Each morning I go on a walk with my dogs on the property. I walk while synchronising the rhythm of my breath with my steps, I count four steps while inhaling and four steps while exhaling and I repeat this process. I acknowledge that I am walking while observing the nature and my dogs running around attracted by smells here and there. Therefore, I am perfectly conscious of my body walking and the beauty of the nature around me, of the air entering my lungs and of the calm and harmony taking place within me, but analysis in not part of this exercise. Only silence exists within me. I am like a driver steering a machine looking through the windows that are my eyes. I see what is happening while being independent from the action itself.

This is a marvellous moment during which all worries of life are set aside, opening a space for the current moment in all its perfection. This walk lasting about 45 minutes represents a moment of complete rest and a total reenergising of my entire mind and body. This type of promenade can take place anywhere, even during a short period in a hallway in the building where you are working when you go from one room to another or on the street while going somewhere walking. Experience this when going to a meeting. Walk while reciting your favorite mantra in your head or simply while counting your steps or becoming aware of your breathing without analysis. This exercise allows you to distance yourself from issues that you will have to face later on and opens the door to peace and harmony. Upon arrival at your destination, you will be relaxed and ready to confront any issues that may arise.

LAYING DOWN POSITION

> *"Even during the deepest sleep, you must remain aware of the void."*
>
> *Golden rule of meditation*

Those practicing meditation for a long time and who have succeeded in dominating their physiological impulses can practice this form of meditation without falling into unconscious sleep.

But this is not a recommended position for the beginner since it will automatically lead to sleep. But I wanted to mention it here, because this form of meditation can become a mean to find sleep and eliminate insomnia for those with sleep disorders. Meditation is an exercise which empties the brain of all thoughts interfering with sleep. It is certainly the best sedative in existence and it is not habit-forming as pills can be.

OTHER POSITIONS

> *"Meditation is a discipline allowing rising walls of will making it possible to ignore the invasion of thoughts and to live in harmony with self and others."*
>
> *Paramahansa the Kagyütpa*

To end this chapter, I must insist on the fact that meditation can be practiced in all possible positions (postures) and at any moment without discrimination, depending on the concentration capacity that one has reached through practice.

The objective is to meditate as often and as long as possible. It is clear that in the beginning this will require great discipline, but with repetition and time this state will become natural and it will become easy to keep aware of what is happening inside and outside of your mind, during mundane activities, without necessarily falling into bipolar analysis.

Let us recall that **the practice of meditation comes down to living the current moment (NOW) without analysis** of any kind. To meditate while eating, one only eats while being aware of eating exclusively of any other thought, without analysis. To meditate while walking, one walks while being aware of walking and nothing else, without analysis. And it is the same for any other situation met during one's day. One has to become an observer not an analyst.

ACKNOWLEDGING WHAT IS MEDITATION

"A good meditation system generating the power required to concentrate the mind on only one thought is essential to succeed."

The twelve indispensable things
Meditation precepts

Prior to begin meditating one must understand what meditation is. We will establish a few criteria that will allow us to see the difference between various states of reflection or meditation.

Meditation is the capacity to ignore the thought process and to abstain from analysis, thus if you think, if you are analysing, if you are reflecting on something you are not meditating. Meditation is observation, but even if observation is the path to follow one must not assess or analyse what one is observing. It is permitted to identify but not to analyse. Any form of analysis sets in motion a mental and intellectual process that is based on bipolarity, therefore, it is automatically erroneous, contaminated due to its tendency to classify everything resting on comparison, evaluation and analysis of previous life experiences. **The only real thing is silence reached through the abstraction of the thought process, and this is what we are looking for.**

You must become a neutral observer without objective or perspective.

You see a horse, thus a horse is a horse that is a horse, nothing else and one's attention can go on to something else that is only what it is.

Meditation is the concentration of one's attention on a point, word, sound, void, breathing, etc., without being disturbed by the thought process. Then one may reach this state where it is possible to be no one in particular, but to be conscious that one is the whole universe.

We must become the essence, the fruit, the beginning and the end, to be and not to be. We must be what we are, the observer and the observed, the reality creator of the illusion and creator of the reality.

THE DISCOVERY OF SILENCE

"As soon as thoughts become quiet, silence sets in and the illusory world just disappears."

Golden rule of meditation

Most people do not know and never experience the inner silence. Can you imagine thinking of nothing, evaluating nothing, criticising nothing, nothing to love or hate. Experiencing only the all-embracing silence that invades all levels of what is no longer the everyday distracted awareness, but the pure and clarified consciousness of meditation.

People in general believe that the fact of thinking is life, consciousness, that their overall baggage of thoughts constitutes them. The overall baggage of thoughts is nothing and no one. Our thoughts as a whole are the accumulation of the successive bioelectric fluctuations of our brain reacting to the exterior stimuli, to our actions and reactions as well as those of others in our environment.

The first moment of higher awareness that you will experience will be to realize that you exist, that you are still conscious of being even when you stop thinking. That thoughts are not the real you, you are something totally different. Every being is consciousness.

Take a long breath through the nose while concentrating on the path of the air, then when your lungs are full let the air out while following its path out, without thinking of anything else.

When you reach the end of the exhalation, be attentive, and you will realize that you are not thinking of anything. You will experience an inner emptiness, silence in your head, this will last only a few seconds, you will have been in a state of meditation for a few seconds, then practically immediately, surprised by this state, your brain will enter into an analytical phase comprised of a more or less extended period of evaluation of the situation (experience) in order to classify the event within a known context. From the instant the brain enters into play and realizes this state of silence, meditation is over, and you are subjugated by thoughts. Therefore you are not in control of your body and brain anymore, since thoughts (aggregates) are giving the orders at this point in time. Repeat this experience several times, taste these few seconds of silence to familiarise yourself with this state and understand that even in absence of thoughts you still exist, you are still present and conscious.

These instants of precious silence are what you wish to perpetuate for as long as possible. This is the silence that great wise men of the world call quiescence, the instant of ultimate peace, the unparalleled refuge where human beings can take shelter from the impact of the daily life, away from the invading, disturbing and often painful thoughts. It is also in this state that the ultimate truth will illuminate your presence, you will experience moments of pure happiness and unlimited knowledge.

Padma Sambhava, a great Wiseman said, "one second of inner silence is worth thousands of years of noisy life." Thus you must be patient during the practice awaiting you, since each instant of silence is a success without parallel, a victory that will bring you peace, harmony and the capacity to see the world with an improved vision.

During meditation, when you become aware that the thoughts are taking over your consciousness and that they are as usual performing their crazy dance of emerging and immersing ideas, you just acknowledge their presence and let them vanish out of your mind and come back without tension to your concentration and to the inner silence, without losing patience, without becoming nervous.

"With time, within the inner silence, you will discover the real face of truth and reality."

ABSENCE OF FORCE

"Be at ease in your body, do not give or take anything, the mind and body are at rest."

Tilopa

One must not at any time apply force to the concentration of the attention. One does not concentrate by frowning. One must be relaxed at all times and keep calm even when confronted by the endless emergence of thoughts disturbing the purity of attention. Force, impatience or nervousness can only increase the emergence of thoughts. You must remain calm, relaxed, aware and alert.

Moreover, any force applied during meditation can cause mental tensions and headaches, which are not desirable when one wishes to reach calm, peace and harmony.

A successful meditation proceeds in a state of relaxation of body and mind when the attention is inflexible from its focus.

"As the leaf accepts the whims of the wind while remaining attached to the branch, the attention must bend to the whims of the thought process without being distracted from its source of attention."

MEDITATION USING BREATHING (SILENCE)

> *"Emptiness has no need for support, MahaMudra rests on nothing, without any effort, while remaining relaxed and natural it is possible to break the yoke and to reach liberation."*
>
> *Tilopa*

Meditation with the help of the breathing process is certainly the simplest and most flexible method that one may practice. The focus of the attention on one's breathing can be practiced anywhere and at any time of the day.

The practice of following the path of our breathing allows one's attention not to be disturbed by thoughts. You will need some patience and tolerance to ignore the frustration at the beginning before tasting the fruits of your first success.

The attention, this inner view, remains neutral and you must focus your attention on the movement, rhythm of your breath. In this state count one (1) while inhaling, then two (2) while exhaling slowly, without forcing the breathing one way or another. Continue this exercise up to ten (10) times without distraction, totally concentrated on what is happening, without analysis, evaluation or measure, when you reach ten, restart at one (1) and carry on.

During this exercise the eyes can remain closed or opened. If your keep them closed, they will focus on nothing in particular and if they are opened they will be focussing on something (a simple object) 5 to 6 feet away (1.5 to 2 meters) in front of you. This object of focus and attention can be almost anything, a small stone, a piece of wood, anything simple that will not prompt the mind to enter into an analytical phase.

At the start of such practice, you will feel that it is impossible to reach the desired inner silence, since so many thoughts will invade your consciousness.

Do not lose patience, this is a normal experience and inner silence and peace will come shortly with time and practice.

Silence exists when one can ignore the thought process, when one becomes immune to mental images. If those images do not affect us anymore, if the noise of analysis becomes silent, then we are meditating, we are in a state of peace, calm and introspection bringing us the inner harmony that we are looking for and finally the ultimate truth.

TECHNIQUE OF BREATHING DURING MEDITATION

> *"While maintaining body and mind tranquility, concentrate your attention on each inhaling and exhaling of the air to and from your lungs exclusively of anything else."*
>
> *Nirvanic path*

Breathing used to focus the attention during meditation must not be too deep or too shallow but it must be complete.

The air during breathing passes through the nose, throat and through the lower part of the lungs toward the abdomen (belly) that rises lightly then the air fills the upper part of the lungs. This is a complete inhaling cycle. One must not force anything; breathing must be natural and comfortable.

There is no special waiting time at the end or beginning of the respiration. You must feel at ease without effort. Breathing must be as normal as possible and you must keep focused on the inflow and outflow of the air without being distracted.

The outflow of the air takes place from top to bottom to empty the upper part of the lungs as well as the whole chest down to the diaphragm that will come down lightly to empty completely. This is a complete exhaling cycle.

Count one (1) at the beginning of the inflow and two (2) at the end of the outflow of the air, then carry on (3), (4), (5), (6), and so on up to ten and start over.

To ensure that you use the right breathing method, place one hand on your belly at the navel. During inhalation you will feel your belly going out a little and during exhalation it will be going in a little toward the inside.

This type of breathing is the one you should adopt in order to take advantage of the oxygenation brought to the body in general. Most people do not breathe correctly; their breathing is too superficial and does not oxygenate their body appropriately.

Take a moment to become conscious of your normal everyday breathing. If it is located in the upper part of the chest, you do not breathe correctly and your body is lacking appropriate oxygenation.

Thus you must practice this complete breathing method by first filling the lower part of the lungs followed by the upper part; this has to become an automatic way of breathing. This breathing, in addition to bringing sufficient oxygen to the body continuously pushes on the diaphragm to facilitate digestion. The diaphragm continuously pushed down by the lower lungs massages all organs located in the abdomen.

In early times masters used to request their disciples to count their breathing up to one hundred thousand. They pretended that this was allowing the disciple to understand the mechanism of breathing and of various other body organs. This was in addition to practicing this breathing method to focus the attention on emptiness with better efficiency.

In fact, one must reach a state of total balanced breathing and of no distraction, thus a state during which thoughts, words and body are totally at rest, where nothing exists but absence of thought, void.

It is important not to become discouraged or impatient. This is not a race to succeed. If you succeed in maintaining mental silence during a few seconds, you have already achieved a great success. It means that you know that the inner silence exists, and you know the objective that you wish to reach. Think about most people living with the relentless noise of their thoughts, without ever a moment of rest. You have the chance at this stage to taste a few seconds of silence and this is already a success. The next step is to extend this period of inner rest (silence).

Let us not forget that the method is the goal and the goal is the method.

MEDITATION USING A MANTRA

> *"OM-Mani-Padme-Heum (The diamond is in the lotus)"*
>
> *Kriyananda*

A mantra is similar to a Christian prayer when that prayer is not a complaint or a request to a superior being. But rather when a prayer is a succession of words allowing one to focus his attention on a sole superior being without thought or analysis.

A mantra is a word or series of words to which you can give a signification or a name. This is not of great importance since the sound is only a tool to support the focus of attention on silence, void.

A mantra is a sound or a series of sounds repeated several times during a certain period while one does not think, does not reflect but only repeats the sound or series of sounds allowing him to focus his attention on this sole sound.

We are always coming back to the same point, any tool allowing to focus the attention on only one thing while disregarding any other thing (thought) is used to practice what is called meditation.

Meditation: absence of thought and analysis. Focus of the attention on only one thing while disregarding all others.

Example of a mantra: "I touch the light" this one is my favorite mantras. I recite it in my head in four steps. But it can be different from one person to another; you can invent your own mantra and recite it while synchronizing it with your own breathing rhythm. The important point is to be at ease with one's mantra and to recite it in perfect harmony with oneself and with a total degree of attention without analysis or reflection.

Here are some examples of mantras:

- I am the essence
- am energy
- I am inner silence
- Infinite light
- I touch the light
- I am perfect void
- I am the universe
- I touch the sun within

MEDITATION USING AN OBJECT

> *"The attention focused on an object, without becoming the object, allows the observer to become the observed."*
>
> *Golden rule of meditation*

It is also possible to meditate while focussing one's attention on an ordinary object. Once again it is not the object or the word or the sound that has any importance because they are only tools focusing one's attention on only one thing.

A simple object is recommended since it will not prompt the mind to enter into an analytical phase. This object will be placed some 1.5 to 2 meters (5 to 6 feet) in front of the meditator. The attention is focused on the object without eye tension (tension will dry the eyes that will become tearful); All thoughts are acknowledged and then ignored and the attention must remain focussed on the object without one identifying to the object. It is recommended to practice this attention-focusing method in association with one's own breathing rhythm. Thus sight is focussed on the object and attention on the breathing rhythm simultaneously.

THREE MAIN STEPS

> *"Keeping the mind relaxed and flexible does not imply to make it insensitive but rather to improve the awakening of its consciousness."*
>
> *Lama Kong Ka*

1ST STEP

During meditation, as soon as a thought appears, one must cut it, erase it, reduce it to nothingness, then return to the original meditation state.

<u>This is the first step that will allow you to realize that it is impossible to eliminate the thought process, or the emergence and immersion of thoughts within your head. The solution to this issue rests in the second step below.</u>

2ND STEP

Do not allow emerging thoughts or concepts to form within your head or do not allow yourself to identify to the emerging thoughts during the course of meditation practice.

During the course of this second step you must recognise the presence of thoughts continuously emerging in your head and let them vanish at the horizon of your consciousness. Without letting yourself be affected or captured by these passing thoughts. As soon as you become aware that you are distracted by a thought, acknowledge its presence and let it vanish, then come back smoothly and without tension to your meditation.

3RD STEP

Practice the art of letting your mind take on its natural state of absolute quietness, not affected by the distracting process of thoughts in emergence and immersion.

You will experience a few seconds of silence, then suddenly thoughts will emerge and invade your consciousness, as soon as you become aware that you lost your focus, you must without irritation or impatience simply acknowledge their presence and come back to the silence focussing again your attention on your breathing, and carry on. With time and practice these periods of silence will become longer, peace and harmony will be more and more present and you will experience unforgettable moments of peace and calm otherwise inaccessible in our ever busy world. This period is known under the name "pendulum", the time during which consciousness continuously goes from a stage of consciousness to one of distraction. One must return to the center and the best method to do so is to refocus the attention on one's breathing. Return to counting your breathing comfortably while keeping your attention focused on the cycle, without thinking, without analysing.

In the song MahaMudra composed by the Indian master Tilopa who is the source of the teaching of MahaMudra in Tibet and who is still to this day the most respected Wiseman in India and Tibet, it is said the following: "Do nothing with your body but keep it relaxed, firmly close your mouth and remain silent, empty your mind of all thoughts. As the bamboo bending to the wind let your body relax completely. MahaMudra (meditation) is like a child's thought, the child does not try to understand or analyse what he is experimenting but only observes and wonders before this inner deployment. Meditation is the attention attached to nothing. While doing this you will reach the understanding of all things."

Caution: It is important during these moments of intense attention focus to ensure that one is not becoming the object of the observation or focus. One must remain awake, alert to all that is happening without becoming enslaved, without identifying to what is happening. The level of consciousness, of awareness must remain neutral and free from any attachment or link. Consciousness is only observing, nothing else, not analysing, not evaluating.

It is well known that the absence of thought presence in one's head maintains mental and corporal calm and thus promotes meditation (inner silence).

BRIEF EXPLANATION OF MEDITATION

> *"To contemplate the essence of truth one requires to wear corrective lenses that only meditation can offer."*
>
> *Golden rule of meditation*

1. Relax body and mind through muscles relaxation and controlled breathing.
   State of calm
2. Focus the attention on only one thing, breath, mental point, sound (mantra) etc.
   State of meditation
3. Reach the inner silence through focusing the attention on only one thing.
   State of quiescence
4. Contemplation of the unity and finally confrontation with the ultimate truth.
   State of understanding

OTHER FORMS OF MEDITATION

> *"Do not think, do not imagine, do not analyse, do not reflect, keep your mind in its natural state, without any distraction."*
>
> *Tilopa*

There exists several forms of meditation and different schools will advise the use of one or other method of focussing one's attention to reach projected objectives.

In fact meditation has only one goal, which is to develop the mental power required to focus one's attention on only one thing (breath, object, word, sound, etc.) at the exclusion of anything else without analysis. This state of concentration will generate higher understanding. Meditation must allow the attention to remain neutral, without attachment, an observer, without being affected by the continuously appearing and disappearing thoughts.

If the meditation method you are practicing does not, in time lead you to your objective, you must try another form of meditation. But meditation will always be what it really is "inner silence".

Furthermore, do not let anybody impose their view to you, whatever it is. Do not listen to fraud attempting to convince you of their good or bad views regarding meditation. You are the master of your own destiny, master of your own decisions and master of your becoming. Any form of meditation must be practiced freely and without any constraint. Anyone practicing meditation must be free to personally experiment the statements of anyone else providing advice or any other form of teaching. If it is not the case, look somewhere else to find what you are looking for.

There are small masters attempting to sell what they believe to be their own truth and there are great masters advising you how to experiment your own truth. Please choose a great master if you feel the need for one.

PATIENCE

> *"The truth will be known to you only through patience and ultimate silence."*
>
> Words of Padma Sambhava to his disciples.

There are several methods of meditation, but there exist only a few qualities to reach the projected objective of meditation. And the most important one is perseverance. This is the quality to cultivate for anyone wishing to succeed where thousands were faced with failure. In silence the observer is patiently waiting and watching his thoughts becoming exhausted and his attention becoming immune to distraction.

The meditator must not become tired or impatient, he must remain flexible and attentive without rigidity, he must remain highly flexible of mind and body. A thought appears, he acknowledges its presence and lets it continue on its way to its disappearance at the horizon of his consciousness without being affected. The meditator must realize that meditation practice, especially at the beginning, is a long and difficult process, but that he must persist in order to reach what he is looking for.

One practicing meditation with fervour and faith will reach the truth, nothing and nobody can deny him this result.

It is usually during the most critical moments, when the will is ultimately weakening, that the greatest experiences are revealed. One must never abandon, one must come back to the original position, close the door to one's sensations and open the inner eye that has the capacity to see all, even the invisible.

Observe without rest in order for one day to see the ultimate light illuminating the world of shadows and confusion.

EXPERIENCES

EXPERIENCES THROUGH MEDITATION

THOUGHT CUTTING

> *"Cut off a thought at the root at the exact moment it instantaneously appears, when it emerges."*
>
> *Nirvanic path*

This first stage will allow you to understand the operation of your brain, namely the emergence and immersion of thoughts.

During the practice of meditation as described above while focusing your attention on the breathing process and counting your breaths appropriately, you will need to try to erase all thoughts appearing in your mind.

You are breathing and counting and all of a sudden, Puff! A thought appears, you acknowledge its presence and you eliminate it, then you return to your exercise.

This exercise allows you to witness the emergence and immersion of thoughts in your mind. To see them appear in your head and then to see them disappear into emptiness (void).

THOUGHT PROCESS

> *"Thought process is the normal mechanical reaction of the mind at work when it reacts to internal and external random stimuli."*
>
> *Meditation precept*

Any thought, any mental image or word formation is due to the interaction of your brain synapses, among themselves or with external stimuli. When one focuses his attention on a particular idea requiring an intense cerebral effort, there arise, without our consent, some bioelectrical interactions between our brain synapses that generates thoughts.

Thus, it is obvious that when one drops his guard and lets his brain act freely, this automatically and infinitely generates unwanted thoughts taking their source in the internal mental process or from external stimuli.

Since our current and past life experiences are stored in our brain, a bioelectrical signal touching a particular synapse will activate the particular memory attached to it. This process can be experienced during meditation as follows: all of a sudden, a thought arises in your brain "I have to buy bread before returning home . . ." or "I must meet this guy this evening at 8 pm . . .", etc. This type of thought or any other is unlimited and they will appear one after the other in your head without you doing anything, indefinitely.

Acknowledgement: Thoughts emerge in my brain and they immerse in it without my will. Thus, thoughts are elements alien to the "ME".

DISREGARDING THOUGHTS

> *"Let them continue their course without falling under their influence and without trying to block them. Meditation can normally continue."*
>
> *Nirvanic path*

It is obvious that while meditating and observing the erasing and emerging thoughts in your head you will quickly realize that we have no control over the emergence or immersion of our thoughts. The only power that we have over them is to ignore them if we wish to.

During meditation based on the breathing process, while being aware of the air entering and exiting our lungs, we experiment the emergence and immersion of undesired thoughts.

Our role then consists in observing all emerging thoughts without being enslaved to them, without analysing them or qualifying them, we only observe them, then we let them immerse into void where they came from. Then meditation continues.

This exercise is call indifference to thoughts. They are there; they appear and disappear without influencing the level of attention on the breathing process.

It is then possible to compare thoughts to birds or clouds passing through the sky of one's consciousness. A bird appears, I look at it (acknowledge its presence) and I let it carry on its flight until it disappears beyond the horizon. Distraction is not touching me, my level of attention is stable, my consciousness observes without analysis.

Acknowledgement: It is possible to ignore thoughts and to become the observer of their dance.

THE GREAT CUT-OFF

> *"Keeping the mind separated from thoughts as the two ends of a broken rope rests on an indomitable resolution to remain alert without distraction."*
>
> *Nirvanic path*

After experiencing the impossibility of eliminating thoughts, because the energy used to erase them generates other unconsciously produced thoughts, there comes a time of indifference to thoughts that can carry on their dance without influencing the level of attention focused on the target. But there remains a last phase that will determine the success or the failure of the meditation adventure.

After becoming familiar with the thought process, after becoming aware of their source and their impact, after realizing that the elimination of thoughts only generates other thoughts, and that the fact of ignoring them does not stop their formation, it is time to ignore them totally.

The meditator takes a final and irreversible decision, the GREAT CUT-OFF. Master Tilopa reminded his disciples that this action was like breaking a rope in two pieces. As the two ends of a broken rope are separated from each other, the observer is alien to thoughts appearing and disappearing in front of his mind's eye.

The observer (you) does not observe anymore, the observed (you) does not exist anymore. The mind then rests in its natural tranquil state. Nothing can alter it, nothing can distract it, IT IS. YOU ARE!!! Since this is the real ME.

Then and only then is reached the level of attention without fault, the state of quiescence.

Saraha, a Brahman from birth in India and master of meditation, describes this state as follows: "the art of keeping the mind exempt from any mental operation, the act is similar to the breaking of a rope".

Acknowledgement: Tranquillity is the absence of thoughts.

SILENCE

> *"Silence possesses the characteristic of what does not really exist, of what is not linked to the dream or fiction of the illusion of the created world. Silence only is."*
>
> *Golden rule of meditation*

The fact of becoming aware of the silence during meditation means that you analysed the fact of not thinking (analysis is a thought process). As soon as you become aware of something, you are not meditating anymore. You are analysing. Meditation is absence of realization, meditation is only observation.

Thus as soon as you realize that such an experience has occurred you must refocus your attention on the breathing process to continue meditating.

The meditation method using the focus of the attention on the breathing process must take place without effort, smoothly and naturally.

One must follow the path of the air entering through the nose, passing by the upper lungs then the intermediary lungs down to the diaphragm, then the air pushes the belly lightly toward the exterior and then takes the inverted path to exit the lungs through the nose.

The rhythms of the air entering and exiting the lungs, the lifting and sagging of the chest are part of a whole under observation and not under analysis.

Peace and silence take place within what we call the inner refuge (state of quiescence). This place where nothing and no one can reach you. There, in this place, where you alone can access.

Acknowledgement: Any realization of an experience during meditation destroys the truth of reality.

ILLUMINATION

> *"In the state of quiescence the meditator transcends his personality and his microcosmic consciousness breaks its attachments and unifies with the universal macrocosmic consciousness."*
>
> *Samadhi Yoga*

A state of higher awareness (illumination) is not easy to describe since in reality it takes place at the border of the space-time that we know, just between the silence of void and the analytical consciousness. An illumination usually takes place during a state of deep meditation. A the moment of its appearance in the sky of one's inner void there is no sensation and there is not consciousness as such, since in order to become aware that something is happening we have to start the analytical process which allows to identify and classify what is happening, this is no longer meditation but a state of evaluation and analysis.

Thus, we become aware of an illumination when the mental process comes into play and analyses what is happening. The understanding that we can derive from this experience happens at that exact moment of consciousness, since this state cannot last because the analysis taking place is based on the duality of our bipolar world and destroys any form of reality. The illumination happens just one moment before the analysis begins, just before the identification between void and consciousness.

In the following lines I will try to give you an idea of what is an illumination experience, an instant of limitless understanding of the universe. "I am in deep meditation, this means that I have no body feelings and that have no contact with the exterior world. Silence is everything; my non-analytical consciousness exists in suspension within the inner void and silence of the deep meditation state (state of quiescence). This refuge, this space without border where nothing exists besides consciousness, a state of consciousness that is just being. A consciousness that only IS.

Then all of a sudden I experience something like a state of higher awareness that I am the universe, that the universe is me, that everything in the universe is in perfect balance, that everything is OK. I am invaded by this warm empathy for all that exists. I am filled with happiness and well-being. In that instant I know that I understand creation, this illusion that we believe reality emerging from the universal consciousness which is in fact all of us united. This experience lasts only a few seconds just before the coming into action of the thought process. Since I notice what is happening means that my mental analytical system is in operation. And it is from this moment on that I can observe the analytical process destroying the purity, the reality and the serenity of the moment of truth through the analysis of what just happened and the classification of the whole experience in some file within my brain. During the whole process I can feel the truth and the reality becoming mundane, trivial, losing its light, its magic and become ordinary and bipolar."

An illumination experience is an instant during which one succeeds in understanding the essence of creation and in acknowledging the immeasurable beauty of its unity. This is a moment during which it is possible to understand that we are all ONE and indivisible.

TOLERANCE

> *"When a young pregnant girl accused Master Hakuin Ekaku to be the father of her child, in front of the accusing relatives he answered Haa so!. When the baby was born he took it under his protection and treated it with love as if the child was his own until one day the young girl confessed to her parents that she had lied. When the relatives came to apologize, ask forgiveness and take back the child, Hakuin said Haa so!"*
>
> *Jon Winokur*

Half of the world in general does not agree with what the other half of the world does or believe. People would like to change their neighbours to make them act like them, to make them think like them. Half of the humanity would like to dominate the other half. Nobody believes that others are doing things the right way, the world in general criticises and is disappointed by the actions of his fellow beings.

Meditation will bring tolerance since it will allow you to understand that nothing is really bad and that nothing is really good, everyone has his own version of what should currently be good or bad.

Anyone practicing meditation looks around and sees that nature does not include any notion of good or bad. Nature only does what it has to do for the survival of nature. Everything is happening as it should, everything is in equilibrium. Everything is action and reaction.

Meditation allows us to accept what is currently happening and opens the way to new understandings. It allows us not to accept or deny anything, but to see things for what they are in their nudity. Meditation allows us to accept the material world for what it is, as it is, the mirror image of the individual mind on the surface of the infinite sea of the universal mind.

Meditation gives us the opportunity to better understand the world and to more easily accept our fellow human beings.

When someone has the capacity to look into the mirror of the infinite void, that person understands that nothing in the universe can be alien and that everything rests on the same universal foundation.

A single glance on the void teaches us that we are all ONE in our world of illusions and disillusions.

The meditator looks within his inner self to understand that he is only the reflection of his neighbour and that his neighbour is nobody else but his own reflection.

From then on it becomes easier to be tolerant since it is always easy to be tolerant with oneself and with the whole world when one knows that it is what we all are. The WHOLE is in ME and I AM in the WHOLE!!!

PROBLEMS

DISTRACTION

> *"When the attention is under the control of thoughts it wanders in all directions.*
>
> *When it is freed; it remains quiet and motionless."*
>
> *Nirvanic path*

Distraction can come from only one source—Weakness of concentration. But do not believe that reinforcing concentration means to apply more physical effort. This has nothing to do with it. Concentration has nothing to do with frowning.

Solution 1: Refocus the attention on the breathing process. Use an aide to concentration, an object, if the breathing process does not help you. A mantra may also help you keep the right level of attention. You are the only person capable of finding the meditation method most suited to you.

Solution 2: Do not interfere with emerging thoughts. Do not try controlling them one way or another. They must sail through the sky of your inner void (silence) without affecting you, without affecting your level of attention on your medium of concentration (breathing process or other). They emerge from the void and they will immerse in the void without influencing you.

FATIGUE (SLEEPINESS)

> *"If you feel tired raise your eyes and look farther away without distraction."*
>
> *Nirvanic path*

We are talking about fatigue due to work, stress, responsibilities or lack of sleep, and of the fatigue caused by the focus of one's attention on only one thing.

It is obvious that the causes for fatigue (tiredness) listed above will have an impact on the quality of your concentration. Thus ensure that you are not too tired before going into meditation.

Fatigue caused by meditation rests mainly on a too comfortable or a too uncomfortable position, lack of attention or too many distractions.

Solution: Focus on a point some distance away from you, straighten your body in a balanced seating position which promotes wakefulness and alertness.

HALLUCINATIONS

> *"Any image or form is only the expression of one's mental process; the mind does not rest on forms and thus is empty by nature. But even empty it manifests all things."*
>
> *The vow of MahaMudra*

Remember that any thought, any image, any idea or any analysis is the product of our bipolar universe via our thought process, thus biased. All hallucinations or visions are part of the illusory baggage in which we live and does not contain any form of reality. Hallucination is based on analysis and the tainted understanding of the phenomena that we perceive.

Anything that we can perceive through analysis during meditation must be ignored. Since just behind perception is bipolar analysis.

Only void (silence) is reality and only void can generate the truth (reality) but as soon as we perceive that we understood something or saw something we must realize that this understanding, this vision following the initial perception is only due to an analysis. From this very moment the perception is contaminated and no longer represents pure reality.

Thus an illumination, a moment of perfect understanding only lasts for the first instant of the realization or the perception, and everything following this moment is only analysis and classification that are part of the bipolar and illusory world.

Solution: Remain indifferent to any mental manifestation during meditation and remain in a state of perfect attention.

ANALYSIS

> *"Do not imagine, do not think, do not analyse, do not reflect. Keep the mind in its natural state."*
>
> *Tilopa*

It is easy to fall for the analytical trap since our entire life is based on this exercise. Analysis is part of the bipolar world and cannot in any case give positive results during meditation and even less lead to the ultimate objective. Analysis is in fact the intellectualisation of an experience, thus an interpretation based on erroneous data since this data is part of the illusory world of interpretation.

Any analysis based on false data cannot deliver the truth. Analytical data can only come from our past and current experiences and these experiences are the subject of an interpretation based on intellectualised past that is resting on past experiences also intellectualised and son on and so forth.

Therefore we must avoid analysing anything; one only has to observe without analysis. It is allowed to identify without filing because in order to file data, it has to be analysed. We become observers and observed. And when the observer and the observed become a unique entity, the objective (if such objective exists) has been reached.

Understanding: Analysis is illusory and bears only erroneous results.

CLOSING REMARKS

YOUR WISDOM IS YOURS, NOT THAT OF SOMEBODY ELSE

> *"Do not think about the past. Do not think about the future. Do not think that you are currently meditating. Do not consider the void as if it is nothing."*
>
> *Nirvanic path*

It is very important to understand that your wisdom is your own and nobody else is. No one can supply you with wisdom. Wisdom is an individually developed personal affair. It does not come from the outside, it comes from your inner self and it is possible to develop it through meditation.

This does not mean that you cannot ask for help; look for advice from those who already have had experiences more advanced than your own. Take and accept advice, but once alone you must experience it, experience it yourself, and make it your own truth, do not accept any advice without putting it to your own test.

Only one real master exits and he is residing within you!

MEDITATION IS A PROBLEM-SOLVING TECHNIQUE

> *"At the beginning the meditator will feel that his mind spins and swirls like a water fall; at mid-course it is running like a quiet river; at the end it is a vast ocean where the light of the positive and negative are fused into one."*
>
> *Tilopa*

In fact meditation is a technique allowing one to solve his personal problems. Meditation allows one to look upon his everyday problems in a detached manner and to understand that they have only the importance that we give them.

Anyone who can ignore his thoughts has no more problems; those are automatically relayed to another world. When coming out of meditation most problems have lost their emotional charge that was used to dramatize them and it is then possible to confront them with a lot more confidence and to solve them.

Meditation allows one to reach a state of detachment from worldly things without cutting the meditator from what is considered important and necessary in daily life.

REASONS TO MEDITATE

> *"After obtaining a free body it would be regrettable to spoil one's life in useless pursuits."*
>
> *Yogic precept*

It would be impossible to list the thousands of reasons to meditate, whether physiological, mental or spiritual, but it remains that it is important to seek the benefits of meditation for anyone looking to improve his understanding of life.

Meditate for any reason,
BUT MEDITATE!

Sherrington
17ᵗʰ January 2012

The author currently lives with his wife Diane in the peaceful village of Sherrington in the Montérégie region of Québec. Julien writes and sculpts, taking his inspiration from meditation

BIBLIOGRAPHY

Discoveries through meditation
Trafford Publishing 2011

Zen to go
Penguin Books Canada Limited, Markam, Ontario 1989

Guide pratique de la méditation
Édition Arista, Paris, France 1992

Tibetan Yoga and Secret Doctrines
Oxford University Press, London, United Kingdom 1960

Teaching of Tibetan Yoga
University Book, New York, United States 1963

ABOUT THE AUTHOR

During his 45 year career Julien Bouchard travelled to work in several countries in Southern and Eastern Asia, Middle East, Africa, South America and Central America. All these journeys, aside from their professional purpose also served in philosophical and spiritual research in India and especially in the northern part of Nepal.

In addition to studying several civilisations and religions, he has managed dozens of large-scale electrical projects employing hundreds and even thousands of persons. He took advantage of these privileged periods to study the behaviour of his follow human beings as well as his own while confronting daily life in foreign countries and a variety of problems and confrontational situations on multi-ethnic projects.

In the beginning, in his free times, he visited the ashrams of India and some lamaseries in Northern Nepal where he received some Buddhist philosophical initiations. He was actively looking for a simple method of meditation, the purest of them all and the least altered by time and people. In order to achieve this, his research led him back in time in the hope of finding someone practicing an unaltered method of meditation, and finally during a journey in Northern Nepal he met a hermit monk, a master of the Kagyütpa school (an adept of the apostolic succession). The teaching of this guide was based on the MahaMudra (the Great Symbol). One of the oldest and purest forms of meditation known to this day. It would have been stated by a wise master named Saraha as early as the first century before J.-C., and even at that time the Great Symbol was already ancient according to the information gathered in some documents written by the Sage Tilopa dated around the 11ᵗʰ century after J.-C.

The Great Symbol was exported to China from India as early as the 1ˢᵗ century after J.-C., where this discipline took the name Chan, then it was again exported from China to Japan where it is known under the name Zen. Chan and Zen are disciplines based on the Great Symbol, but over time they were subjected to many modifications and additions by various master and practitioners. Thus the Great Symbol is the ancestor of the Chan and Zen disciplines.

It is after all those years of research and meditation the Julien wrote this book describing a simple and effective method of meditation for our times and which can be adapted to anyone wishing to practice the discipline, while trying to alter as little as possible the purity of the Kagyütpa master's teaching.

Julien does not ask the reader to believe or accept what is stated in those pages, quite the opposite. "The meditator must be very critical and believe only what he has personally experimented through meditation."

"Meditation is the best tool ever given to the world. Anyone using this tool can abolish the limits of the created world and see through the illusion shroud to finally grasp what really is our world and the reasons for us to exist within this great cosmic machine."

"In silence, the mind rests in its natural state and in this state it communicates directly with its source. In the silence, the truth makes itself known."

"I wish the reader an excellent journey on the path leading to the ultimate truth. Truth will come in a flash and will enlighten the researcher."